American Habitats

Mountain Animals

Connor Dayton

PowerKiDS
press™

New York

Published in 2009 by The Rosen Publishing Group, Inc.
29 East 21st Street, New York, NY 10010

First Edition

Editor: Nicole Pristash
Book Design: Greg Tucker
Photo Researcher: Jessica Gerweck

Photo Credits: Cover, back cover, pp. 5, 7, 9, 11, 15, 17, 19, 21 Shutterstock.com; p. 13 © Jim and Jamie Dutcher/Getty Images.

Library of Congress Cataloging-in-Publication Data

Dayton, Connor.
  Mountain animals / Connor Dayton. — 1st ed.
      p. cm. — (American habitats)
  Includes index.
  ISBN 978-1-4358-2765-3 (library binding) — ISBN 978-1-4358-3194-0 (pbk.)
ISBN 978-1-4358-3200-8 (6-pack)
  1. Mountain animals–Juvenile literature. I. Title.
  QL113.D39 2009
  591.75'30973—dc22

                                        2008035630

Manufactured in the United States of America

Contents

America's Mountain Animals

Throughout the United States, you can find many mountain **habitats**. A mountain rises high above the land around it. Because of this, the **climate** toward the top of a mountain is often different from the climate at the bottom. A mountain can be topped with snow when the **temperature** at the bottom of the mountain is warm.

The animals that live high up in mountain habitats have **adapted** to living there. For example, mountain goats have thick coats that keep them warm in the cold weather. Mountain goats also have special hooves that help them climb over rocks, snow, and ice.

These mountain goats do not have their thick coats. When the weather gets warm, part of a mountain goat's coat falls off so the goat can stay cool.

Moose in the East

Many mountains in the United States are part of a mountain range. A range is a group of mountains. The Appalachian mountain range is in the eastern United States. The colder, northern parts of the Appalachians have pine, oak, and maple trees. The warmer, southern parts have leafy walnut and **hickory** trees.

Moose can be found in the northern Appalachians. Moose are the largest members of the deer family. They are fast runners, and they swim very well. Moose can be shy, but they are big enough to hurt anything that bothers them!

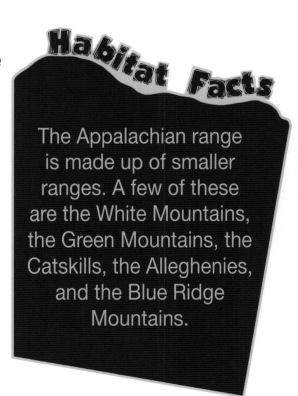

Habitat Facts

The Appalachian range is made up of smaller ranges. A few of these are the White Mountains, the Green Mountains, the Catskills, the Alleghenies, and the Blue Ridge Mountains.

Moose weigh around 1,000 pounds (454 kg), and they have very long legs. This moose's long legs are helping it walk through deep water.

Cougars in the West

In the western United States, there are several mountain ranges. Three of them are the Rocky Mountains, the Sierra Nevada, and the Cascades. The Rockies reach from New Mexico to Canada. The Sierra Nevada is mostly in California. The Cascades are in California, Oregon, and Washington. The climate in the southern ranges is dry, and it is cool and wet in the northern ranges.

Mountain lions live throughout these ranges. Mountain lions are also called cougars and pumas. These big cats generally live alone, using the mountain habitat as their hunting ground.

Animal Facts

A mountain lion hunts animals, such as deer, mice, and rabbits, by creeping up on them. The mountain lion then kills the animal with a strong bite to the throat.

Cougars are tan colored, and they do not have any spots, as some wild cats do. Cougars are the most common wild cats in America.

From the bottom to the top, a mountain is home to many **mammals**. Toward the bottom, there are many squirrels, chipmunks, deer, and raccoons. In the higher parts, you can spot mammals that have adapted to a cool, windy climate, such as elk.

The Rocky Mountain bighorn sheep lives high up in the Rockies. A bighorn sheep has hooves that keep it from tripping on rocks. Male and female bighorn sheep do not live together for most of the year. However, they do come together to **mate**. Bighorn sheep eat grass and other plants.

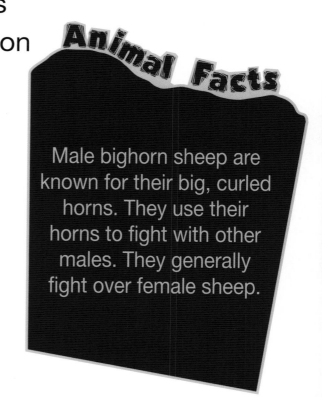

Animal Facts

Male bighorn sheep are known for their big, curled horns. They use their horns to fight with other males. They generally fight over female sheep.

10

Elk, like the ones shown here, move to the lower part of a mountain to graze when winter comes. "Graze" means "to feed on grass."

The gray wolf is a mammal that lives in some of America's northern mountain ranges. Gray wolves live in groups, called packs. The wolves hunt together to kill large mountain animals, such as deer and elk. Wolves talk to each other using barks.

Wolves once lived in greater numbers throughout America, but the spread of people across the country took away their natural habitat. People also hunted wolves until the wolves had almost died out. However, gray wolves are now growing in number. In some places, though, gray wolves are still in danger.

Animal Facts

Despite their name, many gray wolves do not have gray fur. Gray wolves can have white, brown, red, or black fur.

Wolves in a pack are very close, as a family is. Wolves keep each other safe, and they play together, like the wolves shown here.

Birds in the Treetops

Birds are another type of animal that lives in mountain habitats. Bald eagles live in mountain forests, where they eat small animals, such as fish and squirrels. These birds sometimes **migrate** to habitats with more food. However, once an eagle makes a home, the eagle likes to return to it.

The northern spotted owl lives in the forests of the Cascades. The spotted owl lives in trees or nests left behind by other birds. Spotted owls have special wing feathers that allow them to quietly fly down and grab their food. Owls generally hunt at night.

Bald eagles can be seen toward the tops of tall trees, like where the bald eagle shown here is. Tall trees are good places for eagles to roost, or rest.

Butterflies and Bees

Two of the most common **insects** in a mountain habitat can be found in other American habitats and even throughout the world! Bright orange monarch butterflies spend their summers at the bottoms of mountains. As the weather cools, some monarchs migrate as far south as Mexico. This migration can be as long as 3,000 miles (4,828 km)! Western monarchs often migrate to California.

Honeybees are found in most parts of the world. In the Appalachians, you might see them flying around mountain flowers like dogwood and laurel. Honeybees then feed on the flowers. They also make honey in their hives.

Here you can see a monarch butterfly sitting on a purple flower. Monarchs like open spaces, so they can often be seen in mountain meadows and fields.

Snakes!

Snakes are part of a mountain habitat, too. The Sierra Nevada has the Sierra mountain kingsnake. This kingsnake has orange, black, and white bands on its skin. Sierra mountain kingsnakes can be found lying in bushes, under rocks, or around the bases of trees. This is where they wait to catch other **reptiles** and mice to eat. Kingsnakes kill by **squeezing** their food until it stops breathing, and then they eat it whole!

There are some other snakes that live in the mountains. You may spot a black rat snake or a common garter snake creeping along the ground.

This is a northern ribbon snake, a type of garter snake. These snakes can be found on the edges of mountain lakes and streams.

What's in the Water?

Mountain habitats have ponds, lakes, and rivers where many animals can be found. The wood frog is an **amphibian** that lives throughout Appalachian mountain forests. The wood frog is light brown with a dark mask around its eyes. It feeds on bugs near small pools of water. This is also where the female wood frog lays her eggs in the spring.

Rainbow trout live in the mountain rivers of the Cascades. Rainbow trout eat bugs and small fish. These bluish green fish have a pink stripe on their sides. This coloring is what gives these fish their name.

A rainbow trout, shown here, will sometimes spend time in the ocean. However, it will return to the stream where it was born to spawn, or lay eggs.

Keeping Them Safe

There are many other animals that spend their lives in America's mountain habitats, but some of them are in danger. In many mountain habitats, trees are being cut down to make way for buildings. This causes many animals to lose their homes. There are things that you can do, though, to keep mountain animals safe.

One way to help out is to make sure that when you visit a mountain habitat, you do not hurt anything. Keeping the ground and the water clean helps the plants and animals stay healthy. This is something that everyone can do!

Glossary

adapted (uh-DAPT-ed) Changed to fit requirements.

amphibian (am-FIH-bee-un) An animal that spends the first part of its life in water and the rest on land.

climate (KLY-mit) The kind of weather a certain place has.

habitats (HA-beh-tats) The kinds of land where animals or plants naturally live.

hickory (HIH-kree) A North American tree that bears nuts.

insects (IN-sekts) Small animals that often have six legs and wings.

mammals (MA-mulz) Animals that have a backbone, breathe air, and feed milk to their young.

mate (MAYT) To come together to make babies.

migrate (MY-grayt) To move from one place to another.

reptiles (REP-tylz) Cold-blooded animals with thin, dry pieces of skin called scales.

squeezing (SKWEEZ-ing) Forcing together.

temperature (TEM-pur-cher) How hot or cold something is.

Index

Web Sites

Due to the changing nature of Internet links, PowerKids Press has developed an online list of Web sites related to the subject of this book. This site is updated regularly. Please use this link to access the list:
www.powerkidslinks.com/amhab/mountains/